D1708167

Machines in Motion

CONSTRUCTION MACHINES

By John Perritano

Gareth Stevens
Publishing

Please visit our website, www.garethstevens.com. For a free color catalog of all our high-quality books, call toll free 1-800-542-2595 or fax 1-877-542-2596.

Library of Congress Cataloging-in-Publication Data

Perritano, John.
Construction machines / by John Perritano.
  p. cm. — (Machines in motion)
Includes index.
ISBN 978-1-4339-9601-6 (pbk.)
ISBN 978-1-4339-9602-3 (6-pack)
ISBN 978-1-4339-9600-9 (library binding)
1. Construction equipment—Juvenile literature. 2. Excavating machinery—Juvenile literature. I. Perritano, John. II. Title.
TH900.P47 2014
624.152—dc23

First Edition
Published in 2014 by
Gareth Stevens Publishing
111 East 14th Street, Suite 349
New York, NY 10003

©2014 Gareth Stevens Publishing

Produced by Netscribes Inc.
Art Director Dibakar Acharjee
Editorial Content John Perritano
Copy Editor Dorothy Anderson
Picture Researcher Sandeep Kumar G
Designer Rishi Raj
Illustrators Ashish Tanwar, Indranil Ganguly, Prithwiraj Samat, and Rohit Sharma

Photo credits:
Page no. = #, t = top, a = above, b = below, l = left, r = right, c = center
Front Cover: Shutterstock Images LLC Title Page: Shutterstock Images LLC
Contents Page: Volvo Construction Equipment Inside: Netscribes Inc.: 19t, 19c, 24t, 27b, 42, 43 NIST: 36t, 36b, 37 MAN Truck & Bus AG: 25cr Liebherr-International Deutschland GmbH: 18 Hovertrans Solutions Pte Ltd: 26 Herrenknecht AG: 29 Volvo Construction Equipment: 34, 35, 38, 39t, 39b, 40, 41 Shutterstock Images LLC: , 5, 6, 7, 8t, 8tb, 9, 10, 11, 12, 13, 14, 15, 16, 17, 19b, 20, 21, 22, 23, 24c, 24b, 25t, 25cl, 25b, 27t, 28, 30, 31, 32, 33, 35t, 44, 45.

Printed in the United States of America

CPSIA compliance information: Batch #CS13GS: For further information contact Gareth Stevens, New York, New York at 1-800-542-2595.

Contents

MIGHTY MOVERS   4

BULLDOZERS   6

DUMP TRUCKS   12

EXCAVATORS   14

CRANES   16

STEAMROLLERS   20

LOADERS   22

MARINE BARGES   26

TUNNELING MACHINES   28

PAVERS   30

IN THE FUTURE   34

QUICK DRAW   42

Build a Report   44

Show You Know   45

Glossary   46

For More Information   47

Index   48

MIGHTY MOVERS

Humans love to build things. Construction workers build houses. They build dams. They construct highways and bridges.

Long ago, people built structures by hand. It was tough work. Workers used simple tools made from wood, bone, and rock. They made blocks and bricks out of mud and straw. They used animals to move the heavy loads.

Construction machines are so powerful, they can change Earth's surface.

Buildings could not reach for the clouds if it weren't for special construction machines.

Building Gone Wild

Building things is much easier now, thanks to some awesome machines. Dump trucks can move tons of dirt from place to place. Cranes can lift huge steel **girders** to the tops of tall buildings. Big diggers chew up the ground.

What do you know about these construction machines?

BULLDOZERS

Pushing a pile of dirt is much easier than picking it up with a shovel. That is why bulldozers are so handy. Bulldozers are powerful tractors with big blades in the front. With a bulldozer, one worker can push tons of rock or smooth out **gravel** on roads.

Bulldozers can do a variety of jobs, including pushing rocks and smoothing roads.

Bulldozers can work in all types of weather.

Tough Work

Workers use bulldozers in the toughest places, such as swamps and forests. Some bulldozers are so big, they can push away huge rocks from the sides of mountains.

Not all bulldozers are huge. **Landscapers** use smaller machines to clear rocks and trees from yards. Some towns have bulldozers to clear snow during the winter.

Mules and Winches

Who invented the first bulldozer? No one knows for sure. The idea probably came from farms. Years ago, farmers hooked wooden blades to their mules or horses to clear fields for planting. These early machines gave way to farm tractors with steel blades.

Bulldozers can plow vast fields.

In the old days, farmers worked hard plowing fields with just a horse and a wooden blade.

Moving Blades

The tractors with blades first appeared on the job in the early 1900s. These early bulldozers were hard to use. Unlike today, the driver could not move the blade up or down by pushing a **lever**. Instead, there was a hand crank.

Years later, **winches** replaced the hand cranks. The bulldozer driver used winches and cables to move the blade.

Bulldozers became easier to use over the years.

Super Dozer

Some of today's bulldozers are super machines. The most powerful is the Super Dozer. It weighs 157 tons. The Super Dozer, which runs on tracks, has a powerful 1,150 horsepower-engine. But some dozers have huge rubber wheels. Miners use these machines to push piles of coal or to strip away layers of dirt.

The Super Dozer stands 16 ft (4.88 m) tall, 41 feet (12.50 m) long, and 24 feet (7.32 m) wide.

Inside a Super Dozer

The Super Dozer is a complicated machine. The dozer driver needs to know how to operate the dozer's levers and controls.

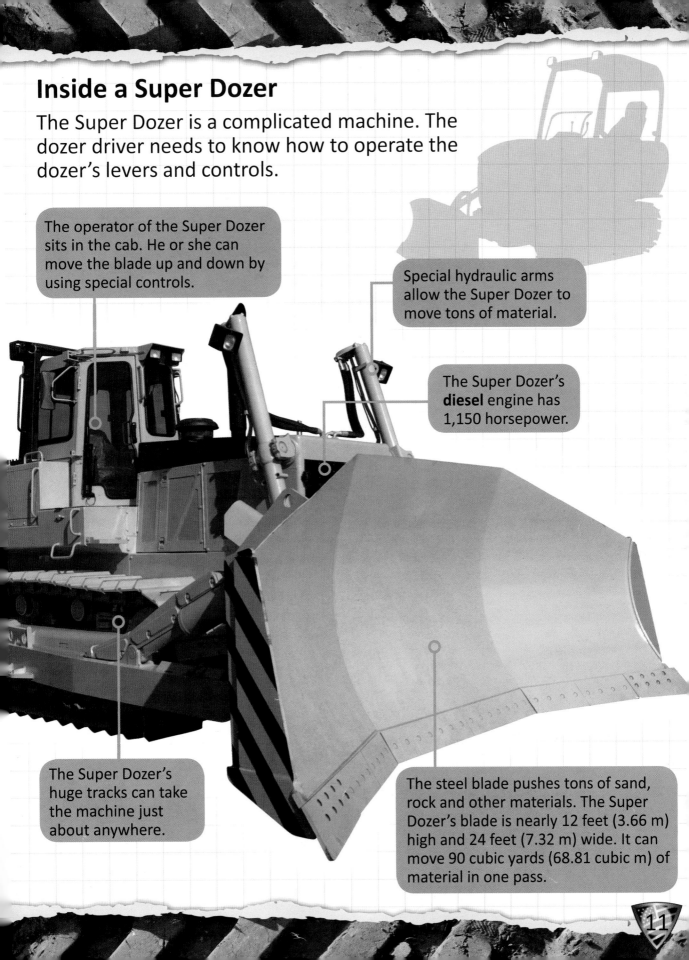

The operator of the Super Dozer sits in the cab. He or she can move the blade up and down by using special controls.

Special hydraulic arms allow the Super Dozer to move tons of material.

The Super Dozer's **diesel** engine has 1,150 horsepower.

The Super Dozer's huge tracks can take the machine just about anywhere.

The steel blade pushes tons of sand, rock and other materials. The Super Dozer's blade is nearly 12 feet (3.66 m) high and 24 feet (7.32 m) wide. It can move 90 cubic yards (68.81 cubic m) of material in one pass.

DUMP TRUCKS

Builders have always looked for new ways to move heavy loads. Long ago, they hauled dirt and rocks in baskets. Someone then got the idea to load up horse-drawn carts.

Workers today use dump trucks. A dump truck is unlike any other construction vehicle. It uses a special **cylinder** to lift the truck's heavy bed so the **vehicle** can deposit its load.

Dump trucks make moving material much easier.

Heavy loads are no match for modern dump trucks.

⚡ POWER ON

A dump truck cannot do its job without **gravity**. When it is time to drop its load, a dump truck can turn itself into an inclined plane. An inclined plane works like a playground slide. It is a ramp. The things at the top slide to the bottom. When the back of the dump truck lifts, gravity pulls the load to the ground. To see gravity in action, you can use a binder or several books to make a ramp.

Next, take a small marble and a large marble. Line them up evenly at the top of the ramp. Use a pencil or a ruler as a gate.

Move the gate away. Which marble reaches the bottom first? Repeat the race several times. What's happening? Gravity pulls on the marbles, forcing each down the ramp. The larger, heavier marble travels faster than the smaller marble.

EXCAVATORS

Excavators are deep diggers. Most have a base that spins in a circle. A huge arm is fastened to the base. At the end of the arm is a scoop. Excavators can dig a hole, swivel, and dump the dirt into a truck or off to the side.

Today's excavators can dig and scoop up tons of material buried beneath Earth's surface.

POWER ON

Knowing the area of a work area is important. Area is the measure of a surface. In a square or rectangle, area is equal to the length multiplied by the width. It can be expressed using this equation:

$l \times w = a$.

Area is always measured in square units. If a worker uses an excavator to dig a pool that is 4 feet (1.22 m) wide and 22 feet (6.71 m) long, it has an area of 88 square feet.

$4 \times 22 = 88$ sq ft (8.17 sq m)

Even early excavators made construction work easier.

Otis and His Steam Shovel

William S. Otis invented the first **mechanical** excavator in 1835. Its name was the Otis Steam Shovel. Its engine ran on steam.

Steam shovels helped dig the Panama Canal. That is the canal in Central America that links the Atlantic and Pacific oceans. Later on, hydraulic excavators replaced steam shovels for this kind of work. Hydraulic power is an improvement to steam power. It uses the flow of liquids and gas to create pressure. It can build enough pressure to help a huge excavator move its giant arm.

CRANES

Why are skyscrapers so tall? How do builders lift huge steel girders and other materials to the very top? They use cranes. Cranes make it possible for the world's tallest buildings to reach the clouds.

Whether placed on the tops of buildings or on the ground, cranes are an important tool in construction.

Towering Machine

Cranes are lifting machines. They use chains, hooks, cables, and **pulleys** to pick up loads. Cranes come in many sizes. Some are fixed to the ground. Others are mounted on top of buildings. Still others are bolted to the backs of trucks.

Getting to the top is easy when a crane is on the job.

Hooked Up

At the center of a crane is its hook. The hook hangs from a cable. It passes through a loop of chain called a sling. The sling goes around the load. The cable runs over a wheel with rims to make a pulley. When the pulley turns, the cable moves. That lifts or lowers the load.

Cranes often use huge hooks and special high-tension cables to lift heavy loads.

Heavy Lift

1 The first cranes appeared in ancient Greece during the fifth and sixth centuries B.C. The Romans made the crane better by passing a rope over a pulley.

2 As the years passed, workers started to use more than one pulley. That made lifting easier. Over time, humans improved the crane. They used winches and special wheels called **tread wheels** to pull heavy loads to the top.

3 Today's cranes are modern marvels, lifting huge loads and putting them down in the right place.

STEAMROLLERS

No one likes a bumpy road or an uneven driveway. It is the steamroller's job to make sure such surfaces are flat. Steamrollers are tractors with huge metal wheels known as drum rollers. These rollers press on surfaces to make them smooth.

Steamrollers got their name because they used steam to generate power.

The operator sits in the cab. He or she can steer the steamroller across a flat area.

Some steamrollers have rear tires. Others have a rear drum that helps press on a surface.

The steamroller uses a heavy metal drum to do its job. The drum turns and is often filled with sand or water to make it heavier.

Compacting Machine

Early rolling machines used steam for power. Today, diesel power moves the rollers. A steamroller has to be heavy. Otherwise, it could not do a good job. To make it heavier, its drums may be filled with water or sand. All this weight presses the surface. Some steamrollers have drums that shake. That helps press the surface. Often the drums need to be kept wet. That is so hot **asphalt** poured onto a road does not stick.

LOADERS

The front-end loader is a construction worker's best friend. The loader can pick up and move tons of dirt and other materials in a matter of minutes. Front-end loaders have many names. Some are called payloaders. Others are called bucket loaders, or bucket trucks. Some are even called scoop loaders.

Did you know?

The L-2350 loader is the world's biggest earthmover. It weighs 258 tons and costs $1.5 million.

Sometimes using a front-end loader is dangerous. That's because when picking up material, the machine might become unstable and tip over.

Scooping It Up

Whatever the name, each loader has a huge bucket that can scoop and move loose material. Bucket loaders can pick up sand, rocks, and other objects. Loaders are also good at removing snow from parking lots and other areas. Most loaders have wheels, not tracks. That makes them fast and easy to drive.

Unlike bulldozers, most loaders have wheels and not tracks.

23

Timeline

515 B.C.

The Greeks and Romans develop a crane like this that uses a crank and pulleys.

1839:

William Otis invents the first steam shovel. It changes the construction industry.

1858:

Louis Lemoine builds the world's first steamroller in France.

1800s–early 1900s:

Farmers begin using steam to power tractors.

1904:

The first modern dump truck appears. It was built by the Mann Company in England. It was called the Mann Gravity Dump.

1920s:

Miners begin using bucket-wheel excavators to move massive amounts of mining waste.

1923:

James Cummings and J. Earl McLeod design the first mechanical bulldozer.

MARINE BARGES

Not all construction machines are found on land. Some work on the water. One of the largest is the hover barge. Its nickname is "Monty." Monty has 8,610 square feet (799.98 sq m) of deck space. It can haul 450 tons of cargo.

Hover barges do not sit on the water—they hover on a pillow of air. In fact, Monty's four diesel engines can lift the barge 4.99 feet (1.52 m) into the air. Monty can glide over snow and ice during the winter.

SR3208E

Barges are important machines that move heavy construction equipment and loads on the water.

Some barges have powerful engines that allow the ship to move on the water.

POWER ON

Barges are big. So, why don't they sink? Archimedes had the answer. Archimedes was an ancient Greek scientist. He said while gravity forces objects down in water, **buoyancy** forces them back to the top.

To think about buoyancy, find a ball of clay. Drop the ball into a tub of water and watch the clay sink. Now shape the clay into a boat. Make sure its sides are high. Put the clay boat in the water. The clay floats. But why? It is the same clay, right?

An object will sink or float because of its shape and how dense it is. When you put an object in water, its weight presses down as the water pushes up. If the object shoves aside, or displaces, enough water, that object will float.

TUNNELING MACHINES

Ants are good tunnel builders. So are moles. Humans are tunnel builders, too. But building a tunnel is not easy. It is hard to dig through rock by hand or to blast it away with **dynamite**. Big machines called borers do this work much better.

Chewed Up

Today's boring machines have a cutting wheel, called a cutter head, which turns around and around. The cutter head chews through the rock in front of it. A moving belt then removes the broken rock from the hole.

Boring machines can dig tunnels through hard rock in no time. The machines have been around for more than a century.

Pictured here is the world's largest boring machine. It weighs 4,500 tons.

Did you know?

It took 11 boring machines to dig the Chunnel under the English Channel. The machines dug out 8.62 million yards (6.6 million cubic m) of earth.

A King and His Tunnel

One of the first boring machines was built in 1845. At the time, the king of Sardinia, a small island in the Mediterranean Sea, wanted to dig a tunnel between France and Italy. He needed to dig through mountains. His boring machine was the size of a train engine. It had 100 drills. The drills cut small holes through the rock. The tunnel opened 10 years later.

PAVERS

The roadway is black and smooth. The double lines are bright yellow. There are no bumps, ruts, or potholes. How did the road get this way? A paver laid new asphalt on it.

Pavers make highways and roads smooth by laying down hot asphalt.

Simple Design

Although it does not look like it, a paver is a simple machine. It lays down a thick coat of hot, black asphalt. As the paver moves down the road, a dump truck leads the way. The dump truck carries cold asphalt. Workers keep loading the paver with the cold material.

Dump trucks ride with pavers to keep the machines full of asphalt.

Churn and Burn

The paver moves the asphalt down a metal slide. A large screw called an auger churns up the material—much like a butter churn stirs up cream. As the auger spins, the paver heats the asphalt to 300 degrees Fahrenheit (148.88 degrees Celsius).

The hot asphalt spreads out easily. The paver flattens and smoothes it as the machine lays the gooey stuff down. Cars and trucks can drive down the road when the asphalt cools and hardens.

Pavers might seem like complicated construction machines, but they are simple to use.

Workers make sure a paver is laying the asphalt down in a straight line.

IN THE FUTURE

Engineers are always looking for ways to make construction machines better. The construction machines of tomorrow will be smarter. They will not dirty the air and land as much as today's machines do. They will use computers, **sensors**, and lightweight materials to lift, pull, and move heavy loads.

The construction machines of the future will be easier to use, cleaner to run, and able to move heavier loads.

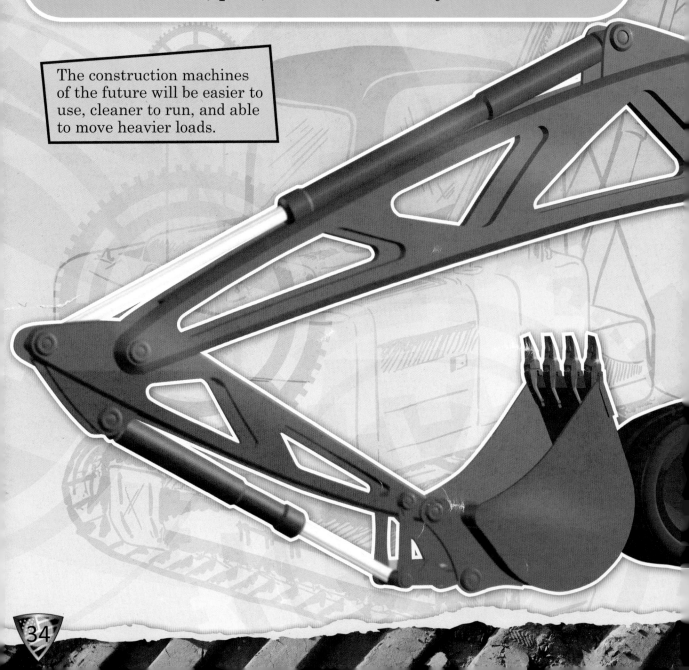

Bigger and Faster

Construction machines have changed greatly over time. The machines we use today are bigger, faster, and harder working than machines from long ago. Machines have changed the face of the planet.

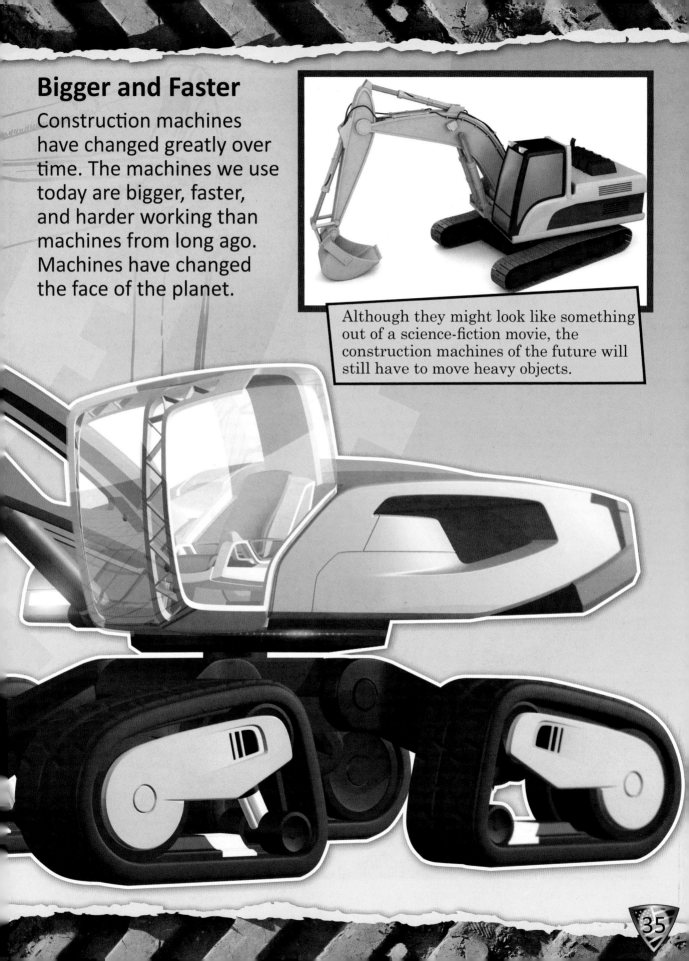

Although they might look like something out of a science-fiction movie, the construction machines of the future will still have to move heavy objects.

Robocranes

The crane of the future is the robocrane. Unlike other cranes, this high-tech crane is made of lighter, stronger materials. Those materials allow the robocrane to lift very heavy loads. It can position heavy loads right where they need to go.

The crane has hydraulic legs and steel cables. Unlike regular cranes, robocranes have tiny sensors that pay attention to how tight the cables are. The robocrane also has a high-tech computer that can change the tightness of the cable as needed.

Robocranes can cut steel.

This model shows how workers use robocranes to put a piece of metal on a ship.

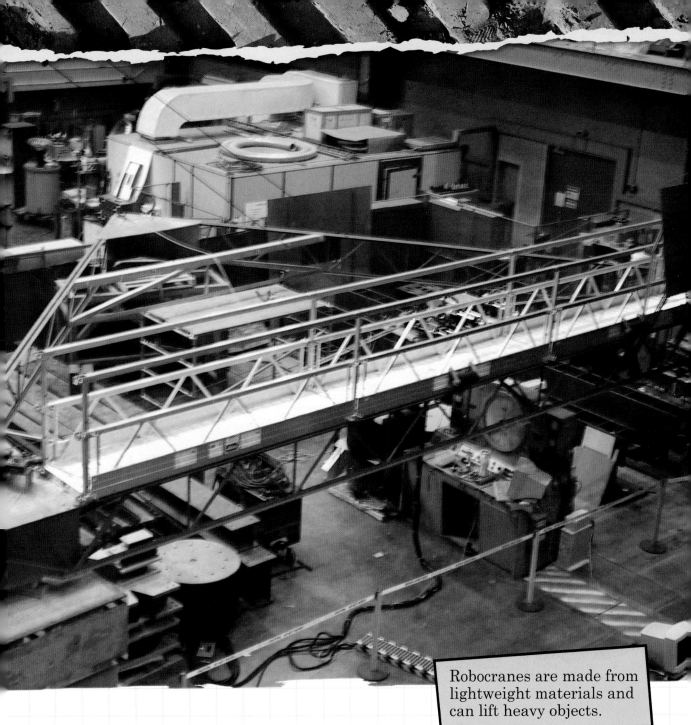

Lift On/Lift Off

The U.S. Navy has a special crane, too. Sailors used to load and unload ships only in harbors where the water is calm. A new type of robocrane allows the work to be done in dangerous waters. The crane balances the load even when heavy waves rock a ship.

Smart Hauler

The Centaur looks like something out of a science fiction movie. But this is no imaginary truck. Engineers made the Centaur to be smart and strong. In Greek mythology, a centaur is a creature that is half man and half horse. In such stories, the creature is very strong. The new truck moves heavy loads at high speeds.

The dump trucks of tomorrow are fast, sleek, and strong.

Right Direction

Computers and gyroscopes help run the Centaur. Gyroscopes are special instruments used to guide ships. They are also used to make sure airplanes travel in the right direction. Now, these special tools can help run construction machines.

The Centaur can be easily transformed from a rock hauler to a log or pipe carrier.

Sun-Powered

The Centaur gets some of its power from the sun. The truck has special parts that can change the sun's rays into electricity. The front of the cab can come off the trailer. Also, the Centaur operator does not have to climb into the cab. Instead, the cab "kneels" down to the ground. The operator simply walks into the cab.

Instead of diesel fuel, the front-end loaders of the future will run on hydrogen, the most abundant element in the universe.

Future Loader

The wheel loader of the future looks as if it works on the planet Mars. Older loaders run on diesel **fuel**. The Gryphin concept model is powered by a **hybrid** engine. Electric motors control each wheel. But the machine can also use **hydrogen fuel cells** for power. Hydrogen is clean when it burns. It does not dirty the air.

High-Tech Glass

Even the glass on the new loader is new and different. When the weather is cold, the glass heats up. That stops ice from building up on the front window. It also stops **condensation**. When the sun gets bright, the windows get darker.

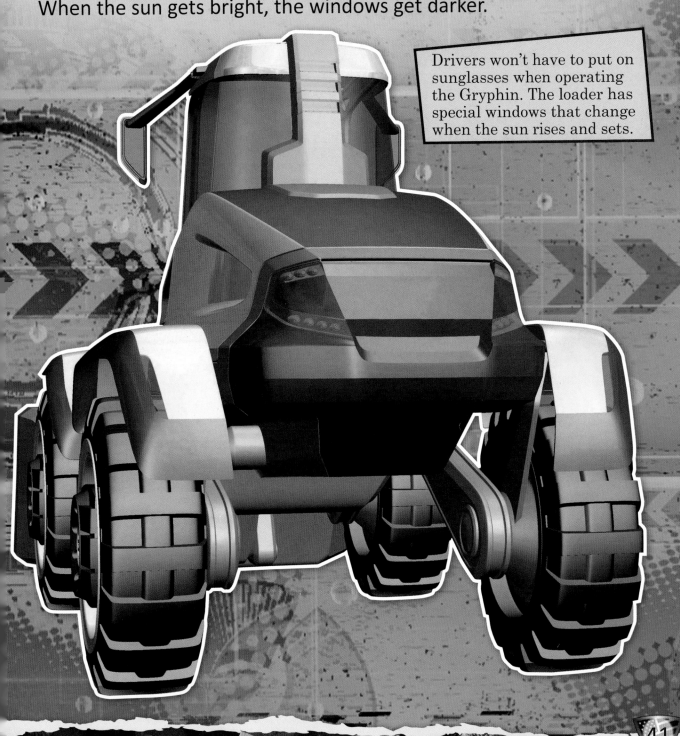

Drivers won't have to put on sunglasses when operating the Gryphin. The loader has special windows that change when the sun rises and sets.

QUICK DRAW

Factories work overtime to design construction machines. Now, you can draw your own vehicle. It will not be as hard, however. Use this activity to draw a dump truck.

Materials Needed

- Paper, graphing paper optional
- Pencil

1

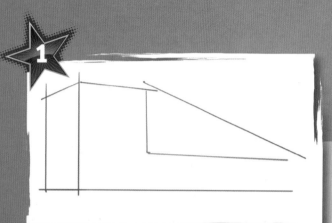

Start by drawing the truck's cab and its bed. Draw the cab as a rectangle with the right side just a bit shorter than the left. The bed should be in the shape of a sideways L. The diagonal line will guide you when drawing the slanted box of the truck.

2

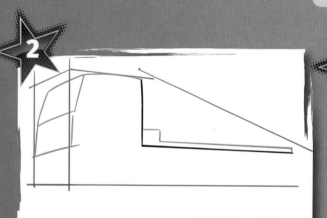

Sketch the truck's front windshield and grill, along with its back frame.

3

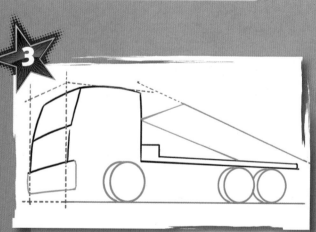

Add the truck's front bumper, front and rear wheels, and the bottom of the inclined truck bed.

4

Add the windows along with the top and sides of the truck bed.

5

Draw the wheels on the opposite side of the truck. Make sure all wheels are detailed to give them some depth. Sketch in a fender just below the driver-side window.

6

Congratulations. You've designed a dump truck.

If you wish, you can add more detail to the truck. Now you're ready to haul a load.

7

Build a Report

How would you like to write a persuasive report? A persuasive report convinces a person to accept your point of view, or opinion. In this instance, your report should answer this question: *Do construction machines harm the environment?*

To write a persuasive article you must use facts and logic. You also need to use examples. Make sure you present all sides of an argument even though you agree with only one. Your report should be in paragraph form.

You can build your persuasive report using these steps.

1. Use this book, the Internet, magazines, or newspapers to support your point of view. Look for facts and quotes that support your position. As you do your research, take notes on notecards, on a computer, or in a notebook.

2. Write the article. It should be four paragraphs long. The first paragraph, or introduction, should state your point of view in an interesting way. The following two paragraphs should use facts to strengthen your argument. The last paragraph should provide a conclusion that reinforces your argument.

3. Look over your report and make sure your argument is clearly stated and supported by the facts. Revise to make the article as persuasive as possible. Correct any spelling and punctuation mistakes.

Show You Know

See how much you remember from your reading. Here are ten questions. The answers can be found inside the book.

1. What type of machine pushes dirt and gravel around?
2. How much does the Super Dozer weigh?
3. Who sits in the cab of a construction machine?
4. What is another name for an inclined plane?
5. Who invented the first mechanical excavator?
6. What is another name for the study of how liquids and gases flow to create pressure?
7. What is usually inside the drums of a steamroller?
8. What material is often used as a road surface?
9. What do all loaders have in common?
10. What is the mythical centaur?

Answers:

1. bulldozer 2. 157 tons 3. operator 4. ramp 5. William S. Otis 6. hydraulics 7. sand or water 8. asphalt 9. a bucket 10. part human and part horse

Glossary

asphalt brownish or black solid material that hardens when it cools; paving material used for road or sidewalk construction

buoyancy the ability of an object to float

condensation a film of water droplets that forms on a cold surface when warmer air comes into contact with it

cylinder an object shaped like a tube

diesel a type of gasoline made for use in heavy machinery

dynamite powerful explosive material

girders long beams usually made of steel

gravel tiny rocks or stones

gravity the force of attraction between two objects

fuel a material that produces power when burned

hybrid having a mix of features, as in a type of vehicle that uses both gasoline and electricity for fuel

hydrogen fuel cells tiny devices that produce energy through changes made in hydrogen, a kind of gas that is part of water

landscapers workers who fix, arrange, and care for grounds or gardens

lever a rigid bar that is used to move or lift a load at one end by applying force to the other end

mechanical of or relating to machines or tools

pulleys mounted rotating wheels with grooves on which belts or chains can move loads in either direction

sensors devices that respond to heat or other agents

tread wheels wheels turned by persons or animals

vehicle a means of carrying people and things, such as a ship, plane, or truck

winches machines that lift loads using ropes or chains wrapped around tubes turned by engines or hands

For More Information

Books

Alexander, Heather. *Big Book of Construction Machines.* Parachute Press, 2009.

Golden, Erin. *Big Bigger Biggest Trucks and Diggers.* Caterpillar, 2008.

Jennings, Terry J. *How Machines Work: Construction Vehicles.* Saunders Books, 2011.

Web Sites

Discovery Kids: Big Construction Machines

http://kids.discovery.com/tell-me/machines/big-construction-machines

Cool pictures are presented from one of the best science sites for kids. The pictures really put the size of these huge machines in perspective.

John Deere Kids

http://www.deere.com/wps/dcom/en_US/corporate/our_company/ fans_visitors/kids/kids.page

This site includes videos, stories, and other activities relating to farm machinery and construction equipment.

Index

Archimedes 27
area 14
asphalt 21, 30–33, 45

barges, 26–27
borers 28–29
bulldozers 6–11, 23, 25, 45

Centaur 38–39, 45
Chunnel 29
cranes 5, 16–19, 24, 36–37
Cummings, James 25

dump trucks 5, 12–13, 31, 38

excavators 14–15, 25

glass 41
gravity 13
Greeks 24, 27, 38
Gryphin 40–41
gyroscopes 38

hydraulics 11, 15, 36
hydrogen fuel cells 40

Lemoine, Louis 24
loaders 22–23, 40–41, 45

Mann Gravity Dump Truck 25
McLeod, J. Earl 25
Otis, William S. 15, 24

pavers 30–33

robocranes 36–37
Romans 19, 24

Sardinia, king of 29
steamrollers 20–21, 24
steam shovel 15, 24
Super Dozer 10–11, 45

tractors 6, 8–9, 20, 25
tunneling (boring) 28–29

winches 19